HISTORY OF

MU~~ा~~~~ाा~~~~ा~~~~~~ा~~, ~~ा~~ा~~ ~~ाा~~ा~~~~

At the turn of the twentieth century, the Manzano, Sandia and Gallinas Mountains were unsettled wilderness areas with no developed campgrounds and only primitive wagon roads and hunting trails traversing the isolated terrain. Resources on the forest were being indiscriminately used by early settlers and in an attempt to manage the land the Manzano Forest Reserve was established in 1906.

The passage of the Land Revision Act of 1891 authorized U.S. Presidents to set aside forest reserves. In 1907, the name forest reserve was changed to national forest. For the next twenty-four years the Manzano National Forest administered land not only in the Sandia and Manzano Mountains, but in the Zuni Range and Mt. Taylor Mountains near Grants, the Ladrone Range north of Socorro and portions of the Alamo Navajo Indian Reservation.

FIRST RANGER STATION IN 1909

1

By 1909 ranger stations were constructed in Mountainair, Tajique and Hells Canyon on the present-day Sandia District. These first ranger stations were not much more than a primitive log cabin with a phone line strung to it for communication and corrals for the ranger's horses and pack string. It was not an easy job for these early rangers, as they were required to provide their own horses and gear and were responsible for a vast acreage of land under management by the U.S. Government for the first time in its history.

TAJIQUE RANGER STATION

The American public was not overly pleased initially with the establishment of national forests. Much of the forested land had been devastated by fire, timber and firewood were being removed at a steady rate and the land had been severely overgrazed by sheep and cattle. The first rangers were to gain control of the timber trade, decrease grazing permits and put out wildfire. Early rangers patrolled not only for wildfire but for illegal activity on the forest as well. Those who had been using the forest often made problems for them and the rangers were encouraged to carry guns to protect themselves.

For a decade, Bosque Peak or El Bosque as it was called in its earlier history was the main observation point for the detection of forest fires in the Manzano Mountains. By 1912, officials on the Manzano National Forest had an operational phone line in service between Bosque Peak and the Tajique Ranger Station. In this pre-radio era, rangers strung primitive phone lines between the ranger stations and lookout points and communicated by phone and also by using flashing mirror signals in Morse code when not near a phone.

Archibald and Alice Rea homesteaded Bosque Ridge in the 1890s and were among the first to settle land within the Manzano Mountains. There was no road to the mountaintop when they decided to homestead the site, so Rea hired seventeen Pueblo Indians and built a wagon road ascending the ridge.

The Rea family established a profitable farm and ranch where they raised cattle and goats and enough vegetables to trade and see them through the year. Archie and Alice lived out their lives on the ridge and their graves remain there today. Since the Rea family had already built a good, wagon road to the top of Bosque Peak, the U.S. Forest Service decided to establish their first fire lookout station on the site and installed a phone line to the location.

According to an article in the *Albuquerque Herald* dated July 19, 1912, the Rea Ranch was helpful in reporting wildfire. "Supervisor Calkins says that the lookout station on the Rea Ranch on top of Bosque Ridge in the Manzanos. . .proved valuable in detecting incipient fires and making possible their extinction before any damage was done."

Other lookout points used by the U.S. Forest Service during this era were Manzano Peak on the south end of the range where a tent was set up for the ranger on duty. Guadalupe Peak on the north end of the range was another lookout point where a pole tower was constructed and a tent supplied nearby for the ranger's cooking and sleeping needs.

FIRST CAPILLA PEAK LOOKOUT IN THE 1920s

The first official lookout station was erected on Capilla Peak in 1922 after the U.S. Forest Service decided to abandon the site on Bosque Peak. Capilla Peak being more centrally located had always been considered the

4

more favorable lookout location in the Manzano Range. Material for a phone line was transported seven miles from the Tajique-Bosque line and a phone installed at the new lookout cabin on the peak.

The first lookout on Capilla Peak was a large, ponderosa pine tree with the top removed for easier access. Juan Chavez from Torreon was the first ranger/patrolman assigned to Capilla Peak. He provided his own horse and rode from Torreon most days and patrolled the peak, glassed for fire while sitting atop the large, pine tree and found and extinguished the fires he spotted. He was the first to staff the small, cabin built in 1922. During this era in fire observation history, the fire lookout was required to find and put out the fires he spotted.

JUAN CHAVEZ—FIRST CAPILLA FIRE LOOKOUT

The 1920s lookout structure was removed in 1963 and replaced with the current lookout station. The lookout cab was transported to the top of the peak in the back of a truck where it was put atop a concrete base already in place. Mountainair District Ranger Bill Buck, Manuel Chavez, Joe Romero and T.J. Archuleta erected the new lookout on the peak.

Also making up land administered by the Mountainair Ranger District are the Gallinas Mountains west of Corona. The mountain range began its history with the U.S. Forest Service on November 5, 1906 when the Gallinas Forest Reserve was created. Two years later, the Gallinas National Forest was combined with the Lincoln National Forest and fifty years later in 1958 combined with the Cibola National Forest where it has remained.

A telephone line was built to the top of Gallinas Peak in March of 1922 by Forest Examiner Burral and Ranger William H. Wood. The first years the lookout was staffed, the ranger/patrolman rode to the top of the ridge each day and glassed for fire but camped at Ranger Tank a few miles to the southwest probably because it would have been hard to haul water for his horse and pack animals. The first lookout structure on the peak was an early pole tower with an outside ladder for climbing to the top.

These early lookouts were not overly safe as described in a June 16, 1932 article in the *Alamogordo News*. "Ranger George Messer, of the Gallinas station, reports to the Supervisor's Office that Paul Porter, fire guard in that district, has sustained painful injuries by falling from the ladder leading to the lookout tower last Saturday. The doctor says he will be able to work in about ten days."

GALLINAS FIRE LOOKOUT

The U.S. Forest Service decided to build a more permanent and safe tower as explained in the *Alamogordo News*, "The local supervisor's office has received notice by the Aermotor Co., Chicago, of the shipment of two steel lookout towers. One is 40 feet in height and will be placed at Gallinas Peak."

The new lookout was erected on Gallinas Peak by Charles Pepper in June of 1933. After he finished with the Gallinas Lookout he erected the second steel tower shipped by Aermotor at the Monjeau Lookout Station near Ruidoso. The steel, lookout tower erected on Gallinas Peak by Pepper is still in use as a fire observation point for the U.S. Forest Service.

****

Article dated June 24, 1972—Albuquerque Tribune— New Mexico Seen from a Fire Tower atop Gallinas Peak—by George Carmack—Editor.

Quick now—without thinking—where is Gallinas Peak? On an air line it's probably less than 85 miles from Albuquerque. Yet, if you know its location—if you know it is in the section of the Cibola National Forest that lies south of Estancia and Willard—you are one in 200 or 300.

Yet Gallinas Peak is a mountain of such beauty that if it were in most states, it would have a state-wide reputation. And the drive up to the fire lookout tower that caps it would be widely known for its spectacular beauty. Yet, it's drive that could be made in ordinary weather by a regular passenger car without difficulty.

Our first objective was the Red Cloud Campground and we reached it around 10:30. This is not a large campground and it had a few improvements but how the simple beauty appealed to us. We chose a camp site in the back of the campground and it was as though we were alone. A man and several boys were around one campsite when we arrived, but they soon struck their tent and left.

We first had a wonderful hike up the heavily wooded draw that ran down to our campsite. There was no trail and in time we left the draw and climbed to the top of the ridge. Through the breaks in the timber, there was a miles-long view across a great valley to another range of lower mountains off to the east.

After starting a fire and cooking our lunch, we took a short nap and then headed to the fire tower on Gallinas Peak. The road was a good one. It had been bladed out and the natural rock made it a good gravel road most of the time. The climb was steady but not excessively steep in any spot. But, what a view—especially with El Capitan off in the distance!

This illustrated something that always amazes me about New Mexico—the unheralded wonders of the state. In the several years we've been traveling over New Mexico and writing about it—nobody had ever mentioned the drive up Gallinas Peak.

In time we were at the very point of the peak—beside the little house in which the fire watch lives—and at the foot of the fire tower. At first I thought there was no one there—and I shouted "Hello." From up in the tower came the answer. It was a woman's voice! Bonnie and I identified ourselves and we were invited to come up into the tower. To greet us we came through a trap door at the top of several sets of steel steps was an attractive, young woman. Bonnie was delighted when she turned out to be another Bonnie—Bonnie Spencer.

And Bonnie Spencer is the full-fledged fire watcher in the tower. This must be one of the most unusual jobs in New Mexico for a woman. There are a number of women who live with their husbands at forest lookout towers during the summer season—but this is the first woman we have met who has this job with so much responsibility on her shoulders.

Bonnie will be a senior at New Mexico State this fall majoring in elementary education. Her husband, Richard Spencer, is also a NMSU senior majoring in ranch management. The Spencers are a summer team in this section of the Cibola and Richard locates the fires Bonnie reports and puts them out. Richard joined us shortly after our arrival at the tower. Both of the Spencers love the outdoors and are thrilled at the job and at living atop Gallinas Peak—with a home with a view matched by few places in New Mexico.

RICHARD & BONNIE SPENCER

****

In the 1960s and 1970s, Manuel Chavez from Torreon was the Fire Management Officer (FMO) of the Mountainair Ranger District's fire crew. Chavez began his career with the U.S. Forest Service in the 1940s when he staffed Capilla Peak Fire Lookout as his father Juan Chavez had done before him. Manuel knew the land well and led fire crews to countless fires without the aerial observation used in current fire locating. Joe Romero, another early firefighter worked with Chavez during these years and many who knew them felt they were the best firefighting and fire locating team in the history of the Mountainair Ranger District.

FIRST SHOP AT THE MOUNTAINAIR RANGER DISTRICT

Bill Buck served as the Mountainair District Ranger between 1961 and 1965 and left behind a memoir describing the techniques used by Romero and Chavez.

District Ranger Buck wrote, "To appreciate the dedication and devotion these men had for the ranger

11

district and national forest, I'd like to repeat what George Schilling my good friend and predecessor told me once.

Manuel was on the lookout and Joe was the smoke chaser at Tajique Cabin. Joe was searching for the smoke that Manuel had called in earlier in the day. It was getting dark and Joe was looking all over. He was climbing trees looking for the smoke drift, he smelled for smoke and listened for the sound of a fire crackling. Hours passed—no luck at all. Joe would drive all the ridge lines flashing his lights for Manuel to see. Finally, Manuel called Joe on the radio and says: Joe do you remember that little fire they had up here, that year when I was in the Army overseas and you didn't work for the Forest Service that year? Do you remember that fire? It was in one of those deep arroyos running off the southwest corner of Bosque? Joe says, Yes Joe I sure do. Manuel responds: This fire is right there, in that exact same spot. Joe drove to the spot and put the fire out. Joe and Manuel were probably the best Two Man Team that I'll ever know."

Bill Buck writes about moving to Mountainair, "When we reported to the Mountainair Ranger District, it was like walking into a new world. We had been at Happy Jack on the Coconino National Forest. We had to leave many friends there when we transferred but it was Alvin Teague who approached me to say goodbye and gave me the best advice I received that day, "Bill don't compare the rest of the forests in this region with the Coconino. The Coconino is not like anywhere else. You are going to join the real Forest now, and you are going to love it.

The Ranger Station was only two rooms with few employees when Ranger Buck arrived. He wrote, "When we arrived at our new duty station in Mountainair there was only one full-time employee there and that was me. The Clerk, Mary Lou Caster, was working two days once a week and three days the next week and there were three seasonal employees. I didn't meet Jim Monighan the Forest Supervisor for nearly four months. A fine man he was. I had called him at the first opportunity to tell him I was in Mountainair and asked him if there was anything urgent going on that I should know about. He said, hell no, just go to work, so I did."

Mountainair Ranger Station in the 1960s

Ranger Bill Buck made additions to his staff and was able to cover more of the required government programs. "I knew that pay rates and the length of work seasons would be critical to the retention of a few key people that we depended upon. That included Mary Lou, Manuel Chavez, Joe Romero and Bobby Meadows.

All of a sudden things were happening real fast. So fast that I don't know how Mary Lou didn't have a nervous breakdown. She had a complicated job. I think whenever she looked out the window and saw Manuel pushing 150 new hires in six different directions, all at the same time. The fact that by the time she got to work, he had already finished his chores made many phone calls required and drove to work. Manuel always stayed ahead of everyone else, and that was his job and he knew it. So all Mary Lou had to do was to look out the window and watch Manuel. The new Job Corps Center was in the plans during these years and there was always plenty to do."

Ranger Buck describes all the changes and activity going on at the Mountainair Ranger District during these years, "There were just so many things happening, and it seemed all at once. There was excitement in the air! We didn't contract any job out to the highest bidder anymore. Every job from planning to completion—all of the work, we did ourselves with local employees. Gene Schmitz, our head contractor was a Bataan Death March Survivor. What a great story he is! Joe Chavez, Manuel's younger brother and his new bride were our first guests in our new home.

**First phase of dwelling—District Ranger's House—
Mountainair Ranger District—1962**

Joe Chavez agreed to relieve Manuel at Capilla Peak Lookout and we went into fire season. In the meantime we designed our best hands to serve as crew leaders in charge of many jobs that we had going. The crew leaders reported directly to Manuel. The heat was on because we must complete every job by the end of the fiscal year.

There were many hired during this time. There was Bobby Meadows, T.J. Archuleta, Joe Candaleria, Wilfred Lackey, Joe Chavez, Carmel Sanchez, Denzel Bates who also owned a gas station, was the justice of the peace and drove a school bus, by golly even George Formwalt the retired postmaster from Tajique and Archie Rea's brother in law. They were all so busy they didn't have time to look where they had been.

BOBBY MEADOWS

We didn't have time recruiting manpower, 75 of them were already members of the newly formed "Los Torros" firefighting crews with three 25 man crews. We had a lot of people coming to work each morning. To avoid traffic jams we just told everyone to report directly to the job site out in the woods. That saved us a lot of headaches. This went on for twelve months. The men were earning their pay and proud of what they were doing. I'd like to add we were also accident free. Equally important was how much they accomplished in such a short period of time. The amazing array of resource jobs that were way over due and it was fun.

We surveyed, we tore down, we built and we even surfaced several miles of road with gravel from a local pit. Sid Wells was invaluable on those kinds of projects. We maintained and rebuilt a lot of miles of boundary fence and we even capped all the old water lines and underground springs left from the CCC Camps in the 1930s. We developed range and wildlife waters and every spring box that needed to be repaired or needed to be developed.

SID WELLS' CREW

Manuel Chavez had a beefed up thinning crew of some thirty men with chainsaws all running at once. Carmel Sanchez was his lead saw man and Joe Romero was the head man, when it came to maintaining the saws. He had a vice mounted on the tailgate of his pickup truck. The sawyers were required to each have a double bitted axe and to keep it super sharp. If anyone had a saw breakdown and Joe Romero could not fix it in the field, then he returned their axe and told them to get back to work.

There were thousands of acres of sapling sized dog hair thickets that had to be released or opened up to the sunlight. Bobby Meadows was the fence man. His crews were hardly ever seen but we could sure see where they had been.

We tore down and completely rebuilt the Capilla Peak Lookout Tower with living quarters. When Manuel Chavez realized that the cinderblock foundation of the tower was not squared he got personally involved.

While T.J. Archuleta concentrated on campground construction—his crews completely rebuilt all the old sites in the Manzanos and then built two brand new campgrounds that didn't even exist before.

One was west of Torreon and the other was in Trigo Canyon on the west side of the Manzanos. Manuel, T.J. and several of us spent many a night in Trigo. It was simply too far to commute to the job. We packed sand and gravel and bags of cement down from the top of the mountain.

I remember having to rent pack animals for the crews. We built retention dams all the way down the canyon, and we built them of cement in order to create small pools of water. Trout are planted in the stream each spring providing a put and take tank.

At the same time all of this was going on, we had a sizeable trail construction crew. We located and built to R-3 engineering specifications the Ox Canyon Trail, the only trail on the southeast side of the mountain. Unfortunately, we ran out of money before the last mile was completed. I was able to arrange for two Boy Scout Troops to come down on weekends from Albuquerque and we finished the trail.

The Mountainair District had a lot of help from the Supervisor's Office. Clay Withrow and Tuffy Swapp were a big help to the crews during these years. Can't forget Tuffy, on the first day we were moving the Trigo Crew over the top and down the west side. Chavez was at the front with his hand crews. Tuffy and his pack string brought up the rear. Now I don't know how soon after Tuffy was born that his parents named him, but I bet he was named before he was born.

On this day as he was lining his pack strings out before heading down into Trigo Canyon, I heard him yell that he hoped they didn't run into that bear as he stared down at a massive, pile of bear scat ahead in the trail. Everyone had to check out the pile before traveling down the trail.

Since the organization of the U. S. Forest Service, there have been people who graze their cattle in the forest without getting permits. According to Ranger Buck, this was happening to Manuel and his brother Joe who had a U.S. Forest Service grazing allotment near Capilla Peak. When they took their cattle off the forest another man would illegally allow his cattle to graze on the same allotment. By the time the Chavez brothers returned their cattle to the allotment there was little grass left for the cattle.

Ranger Buck writes, "I told Manuel to get everyone of our men who had a horse and to meet me at the Chavez Headquarters first thing tomorrow morning. All we had to do was catch one cow, and then we could charge Manuel's neighbor with every one of us riding and every horse that we were riding on. That would include the rent and keep of the horses, mileage and towing to get there and back again. That's for the entire day, even including the time it took to catch the horses in the morning while we were rounding up his cattle and we are going to get an early start.

The Forest Service also had one card that we had never played before. That of course was Tuffy Swapp. I could tell you more about Tuffy Swapp but that would involve telling you about Tuffy's background and his qualifications. We don't have the time or ink and paper to do that here. I'll just say there were about twenty of us who rode that day. Tuffy roped a steer and we held it in our own corral.

When I tallied up the bill it was impressive. I collected the money in the form of a postal money order in the amount of close to two thousand dollars. The strangest thing was that this fella didn't even quibble or complain he just gave me a money order to the full amount. It was made to the U.S. Treasurer.

I sent the case with all the costs, etc. up to Albuquerque. I got a call the next day from Wally Gallaher, Ernie Perry's replacement. I'll never forget what he said. We received your little bomb shell today. Do you realize that's the most expensive cow in the history of the entire Forest Service? I told him I was not aware of that. He told me to give all or some of the money back to him. I said no Wally I can't do that because that would only degrade the authority of a Forest Officer. Besides that, the SOB was quick to pay only because that steer we impounded was carrying another man's brand. In other words Manuel's fine neighbor was a cattle thief.

As the Job Corps construction was revving up I was transferred to Globe, Arizona. We had only been in Mountainair four years but it seemed longer with all the activity we had going. However, it wasn't long before Manuel and I ran into each other again. It was on the Iron Fire on the Globe Ranger District. This was a very large fire and it was running into the Revis Ranch area within the Superstition Wilderness.

I was the line boss. Manuel and Joe were sector bosses and had brought several northern New Mexico Pueblo SWIFT crews with them. About the second day of the fire Manuel and Joe both came up on the line. What a surprise it was to have those two fire hardened veterans with me again. The fire was advancing up slope toward us. We had constructed ½ mile of hand line across a wide bottom through the brush in front of the fire to a point where it was an ideal location to ignite a back fire. I had sent Manuel with several torch men back across the draw. They were loaded with fusees and they had time to do the job.

I had informed the Line Overhead what we were going to be doing and to pull their line personnel back into the safety zone ahead of Manuel's crew. From there we could see what was going on and at the same time stay safe. Once everyone was where they should be, the Division Boss was moving his crews back toward me. I called Manuel's firing crew to get them started. All was going well, but the main fire was heating up and threatening to get to the fire line before Manuel did. As luck would have it when we needed it most, his radio pack set went on the blink! In a panic, I left the rocks and ran up the line yelling—Manuel—Haul Ass—Pretty soon everyone on the line was yelling—Manuel—Haul Ass! By golly he did it!

****

Ranger Buck wrote a column in the local paper. One was found dated June 15, 1962.

This almost is not a Ranger Column. Mrs. Wester called early this morning to remind me that today is the day to have the column ready. I promised to come up with something, but shortly afterwards a fire was reported on the north side of Gallo Peak. I just got back with time to write this.

I'd like to say that without men like Manuel Chavez on Capilla and Joe Romero, Joe Chavez and Bobby Meadows this column might not have appeared at all. At 6:10 p.m. during a strong hail and lightning storm Manuel calmly reported three hot lightning strikes—one, north of Gallo, one west of Sandia Camp and one just inside the timber in Jaramillo Canyon.

This morning, the Gallo Fire showed at 8:45 a.m.—within one minute Joe Romero and Joe Chavez left the Red Canyon Recreational construction job and were on their way. AT 11:10 a.m. they had hiked their way in and were on the fire line. Bobby Meadows followed up with horses and a falling saw right behind them.

Ranger Buck returned to the comforts of his office and to record this story. To me this is a story repeated thousands of times every year in the Southwestern Region. Each fire is always a little different, there's always a touch of suspense. Manuel wonders if the other two strikes will show—and keeps watching. I wonder if I hit the fire quick enough, with enough men, should it have been dispatched differently. The fire season is here and with it a certain excitement.

I'd like to pay due respect to those of you who voluntarily step into the batter's box and take a good healthy swing for this Ranger District in time of need. For instance, on Wednesday, June 6, I was in the field and not in radio contact. Manuel spotted a smoke near Inlow Youth Camp—before he could contact me, a long-time Forest Service employee, Archie Rea called from his store in Tajique and reported the smoke to Ira Caster of Mountainair.

Ira, who for several years served as our district dispatcher stepped right in and dispatched for us until the fire was under control. This is teamwork, mutual understanding, a fine community spirit, a sense of responsibility.

Many of you have "hit the ball" for your national forest. Since my arrival, I can recall George Formwalt, Ramon Lesperance of Tajique, Father Wilkinson of Manzano, Joe Atkinson, Chancy Thompson, Arch Cape from the Gallinas country, Mr. Green at Dripping Springs and the many Mountainair folks who have taken similar action in the past as Ira Caster and Archie Rea did last Wednesday. My sincerest thanks to all!

RANGER BILL BUCK GIVING A TALK TO THE BOY SCOUTS

RANGER BILL BUCK, MANUEL CHAVEZ & JOE ROMERO

****

CLOTA BATES SCHMITZ

The following information was gathered by Clota Bates/Schmitz during her time as the District Clerk at the Mountainair Ranger Station. There were a lot of changes during her years at the Mountainair District. She began her employment in the two-room ranger station to the east and was the first in the present Ranger Station. She has given us a peek into the past!

The following information is what she left behind during her tenure at the Mountainair Ranger District:
Clota wrote, "On February 15, 1965, I came to work for the Cibola National Forest Mountainair R.D. the new District Ranger Verne Greco reported for work also and we were greeted by R.J. Toutges, Ranger Conservationist for the District."

R.J. Toutges, Ranger Conservationist, Clota Bates & Verne Greco

Verne Greco had most recently been stationed on the Apache Sitgreaves National Forest for the past eleven years. Clota was thankful for his expertise on proper administrative procedures. "He assisted me with all phases of my work," she wrote. "His patience was unlimited and his experience was invaluable to me."

DISTRICT RANGER VERNE GRECO

During these years Mountainair and especially those employed by the U.S. Forest Service were excited about the new Job Corps Center coming to town. Clota wrote about those years, "In the meantime, the new Job Corps Center activated nearby and things were quite hectic for some time. Many people passed through our doors after visiting the nearby center. There were dignitaries such as the Press from Washington, along with Senators, Representatives, Regional Forester Hurst, F.S. Pat Murray, etc."

According to Clota's history, Verne attended church and raised four sons referred to as the four-Bs. Bob built planes in Texas, Billie lives in Alaska and builds homes, Bryon works in the lumber business and Bruce is currently a Timber Forester on the Apache Sitgreves NF.

Verne had at first served with the Civilian Conservation Corps (CCC) in his early career and his wife Mary grew up in Vermont and enjoyed researching her family's history and being involved in community affairs. Verne enjoyed working with the Boy Scouts and served as a leader for many years.

VERNE & MARY GRECO

Verne retired in 1967 after a gala occasion at the Job Corps Center, before moving to Taylor, Arizona. Verne and Mary built their own home with materials Mary had continually been hauling to Arizona before they retired. Verne keeps himself busy with gardening, traveling, fishing and hunting.

Clota ended the section on Verne Greco by saying, "Verne's favorite pastime is talking about his family it used to be his sons, now it is his grandchildren. They still keep in touch each Christmas with a letter from Verne updating me on his family."

During Verne Greco's time at the Mountainair Ranger Station was stressful in some ways due to the pressures of the Job Corps Center and the pinon/juniper eradication in the Gallinas Mountains. He projected a dignified manner at all times. Much was accomplished to restore good will and tranquility to the District with those possessing grazing permits and the general public with the Forest Service and Job Corps Center.

****

John W. (Bill) Russell was assigned to the District in 1967 coming from Arizona. He was a young widower with five children ages 5-15. His wife had died in an automobile accident several months prior to his transfer.

BILL & LINDA RUSSELL

Clota writes about getting to know the family, "On a windy day (which was common in Mountainair), I could hear this little voice crying beside the office and when I would go to see who it was, there would be little James

Russell, age 5, crying because he was lonely. With a big hug and the reassurance from his German shepherd dog, he would slowly make his way back up to the hill to his house."

Bill and the entire clan loved their German shepherd dogs, but they did cause a stir among the District personnel as well as the public. One dog especially liked to stay in Bill's pickup (FS) and would not let anyone near the truck. When parked outside the office, the public was afraid to get out and come into the office, George Proctor, Forest Supervisor, warned Bill about the dogs more than once.

Linda moved to Mountainair to teach kindergarten and later married Bill before they left Mountainair. Linda's warm smile and her patient loving attention given to her new family caused us all to love her.

Bill expressed empathy for all of us when he knew we had problems of any kind. He was the most understanding person I have ever known. He shared many of his books and philosophy with me giving me a broader understanding of humanity. Besides the large workload imposed by the Job Corps nearby and then the final closing of the center he had time to be very active in Rotary Club and various other functions of the community.

During his tenure, we moved from our one room office to the new offices built by the Job Corps. What a thrill after being cooped up in a little one room office with supplies and maps stored in the bathtub of our one restroom. I mopped and waxed this little office as part of my duties assigned. We couldn't believe all the lovely space we had, choices over offices and colors of drapes, etc. What Fun!!

Over fifty people attended the Russell's going away dinner at the Golden Grill Café, where he regularly attended Rotary meetings. One of the major accomplishments of Bill's tour was the Range Analysis and PU Studies completed on the Tajique Allotment. This was a critical project brought on by the Tijerina influence on the Region.

****

In February of 1970, George and Ruth Shilling were transferred to Mountainair R.D. This was a second assignment to Mountainair for them as they were here in 1968-1961. They weren't so happy at first, because they loved Magdalena but later enjoyed Mountainair very much. They had two sons, Bill and Lee.

GEORGE SHILLING

George came to Mountainair very qualified, as he had graduated from Utah State in Logan, Utah in 1951. He had previously worked on the Sitgreaves-Chevelon RD south of Winslow, Arizona. He was later promoted to a tree marker on Heber RD. He was responsible for 90% of the Sandia District's watershed. He also worked on the old Gallup RD and Glenwood RD before coming to Mountainair and then Magdalena.

We all enjoyed Ruth popping in and out of the office, and she would rarely leave home during fire season. She loved keeping up with all the radio transmissions and reminded us often if we didn't answer the radio promptly. She was aware of all that went on throughout the District. She and George became very involved with community activities especially the volunteer fire department and Eastern Star. Ruth willingly gave her expertise when we were planning a party or a dinner for the District personnel. We could always count on her to head the committee.

George fascinated us with stories of his "hobo" days and of course his tenure in the Merchant Marines. He and Chris Zamora had many tales to tell of their escapades on the forest. George and I spent many a night recruiting firefighters for the Los Toros SWFF group and getting them off to a fire. Oftentimes Ruth made coffee and kept us company.

George and Ruth's favorite pastime was going out on the lake with their sailboat. As a going-away gift we gave them a radio for their sailboat since George had fallen overboard in a little rough water and lost all his gear. A lovely retirement party was enjoyed by over 75 people at the Shaffer Hotel. George and Ruth moved to Nice, California to be near a lake so they could fish and enjoy sailing.

****

LARRY SOEHLIG TOOK OVER THE DUTIES OF THE MOUNTAINAIR DISTRICT RANGER IN MARCH OF 1974

Larry and Betty Joe were very special to me and Betty Jo promptly adopted me into their family and helped me through some difficult times in my personal life. I was included in family dinners often and Betty Jo and I shared Beta Sigma Phi Sorority.

When Larry was the District Ranger in Mountainair, he upgraded as many of the employees as he could, he also restored our fleet equipment and started building up our fire suppression. Under his tenure, we had a large fire organization, pre-suppression as well as suppression crews. We worked many summer seasonal workers including road block crews. He valiantly bucked the SO as needed to improve the District in any way he could.

I remember Paul Gordon, the Range staff person on the forest telling me that to get along with Larry when he arrived was to tell him to get lost whenever he became a little overbearing about something. Guess what? This worked!

The Soehlig family which included Debbie and Stephen were well liked in the community and when we learned he was offered a job on the Lincoln NF we all felt a great loss.

THE SOEHLIG FAMILY

Coyote prepared the going away party invitation with one of his famous cartoons shown below. His farewell party was attended by over 100 people and Coyote acted as Master of Ceremonies. The community gave them a beautiful painting by our local artist Eulala Snapp.

FAREWELL CARTOON BY COYOTE

Betty Jo and Larry were the first to congratulate me when I remarried Eugene W. Schmitz and entertained us several times before they left our area. They played bridge often with us. Larry tried to add an additional clerk to our staff, realizing that the workload in the office had drastically increased. Part-time help was all we were able to acquire.

During the 5-6 months before we were assigned a new District Ranger, Stanton Wyche served as Acting Ranger. Stan, Barbie, Sylvia and Jimmy lived in the Assistant

Ranger dwelling, because Stan was our District Range and Recreation Staff man. Barbie was employed as the Torrance County Nurse while living here.

****

On October 26, 1975, John and Louise Barntiz from Cheyenne, Oklahoma arrived at our District with their three sons: Jack, Dick and Bill. We soon learned we had a most unusual family in our midst. John and son Bill are bluegrass musicians. John is also involved in woodworking and blacksmithing. Louise is a talented artist and a dedicated school teacher who also enjoys scuba diving for a hobby.

JOHN BARNTIZ DISTRICT RANGER

John continues to delight us with his Virginia colloquil wit. Sometimes we vie to file so we can read his comments made on district copies of letters, reports, etc. He also travels to Madrid for his jam sessions of Blue Grass music on Sundays. He often participates with a music group locally for various fun times.

Under John's tour at Mountainair we have seen several programs initiated. The YACC program for unemployed youths between the ages of 16 and 26, YCC, high school students ages 15 to 18 and the SCSEP for those older Americans 55 and older. We feel these programs have been beneficial to the community and have provided jobs to countless youth.

But, the District feels the most successful program has been with the older Americans. Their expertise, experience and faithful attendance on the job has proved them to be a great asset and many of our targets would not have been met if not for this group. We have five enrollees at the present time two of them are retired Forest Service employees.

The workload increases and decreases according to the limitations handed down from above. In the past ten years we have seen women join our ranks with the fire and project crews, special programs, etc. John Barntiz' term as District Ranger has seen many beneficial programs added to the District.

The last saw log timber sale on the District was in 1974 by Bates Lumber Company. The sale was located in the Ojo la Casa area of the Manzano Mountains. During the summers in the late 1970s we had as many as sixty-five people on board at one time. We are currently contracting the lookouts. In 1984 we added a timber staff position and it was filled by Donald L. Hall from Cheyenne, Oklahoma. He also serves as the recreation and mineral staff person.

****

One last person included in Clota's history of the District is Bob Little. He went by the nickname of Coyote. He graduated from New Mexico State University in 1965 and served as the Range Conservationists on the Mountainair and Magdalena Districts.

He was an outgoing guy who cracked jokes and served as master of ceremonies at Forest Service functions. He had a knack for drawing cartoons that were used on the District Program Plans. He worked hard on range management programs with local ranchers and those leasing Forest Service land.

Coyote, after being out
all night on a fire.

****

October 1984 my job was audited and I was given a promotion from District Clerk to Support Systems Specialist. What a thrill!!! March 3, 1985 another milestone in my life my retirement date.

CLOTA BATES SCHMITZ

One Winter Day we had a visitor at the office who made himself at home in my desk. 1982

****

LIST OF MOUNTAINAIR DISTRICT RANGERS

Thomas W. Carscallen 1908-1912

Llew J. Putsch 1912-1917

Ray E. King 1917-1920

L.A. Shartzer 1920-1922

Louis H. Laney 1923-1932

W.H. Woods, Jr. 1933-1934

John H. Mims 1935-1940

E.W. Cottom 1941-1950

Harlen H. Johnson 1951

Euel R. Nave 1951-1955

Harlen H. Johnson 1955

Harry O. Sontag 1956-1957

Vincent R. Price 1957-1958

George E. Shilling 1958-1961

Bill B. Buck 1961-1965

Verne Greco 1965-1967

John W. Russell 1967-1970

George E. Schilling 1970-1973

Larry A. Soehlig 1974-1975

John A. Barntiz 1975-1988

Susan A. Gray 1988-1989

Frank R. Martinez 1990-2000

Vicky Estrada 2001-2006

Karen Lessard 2007-2015

****

A LITTLE INFORMATION ON THE REMAINING MOUNTAINAIR DISTRICT RANGERS

The Mountainair Ranger District has had twenty-four District Rangers throughout the history of the District. John Barntiz who worked as the District Ranger for thirteen years between 1975 and 1988 has served the longest in that position. Frank R. Martinez served eleven years, Louis H. Laney and E.W. Cottam served nine years each and Karen Lessard served for eight years.

LOUIS H. LANEY 1923-1932

In the first years of the U.S. Forest Service, it was common for the rangers to transfer every few years to help with the building of the districts. Mountainair's first ranger **Thomas Carscallen** served between 1908 and 1912. He passed away in 1912 and is buried at San Marcial, New Mexico.

Ray E. King served as the assistant ranger in San Mateo, NM before arriving in Mountainair.

L.A. Shartzer – *Mountainair* Independent newspaper dated August 14, 1919—L.A. Shartzer, recently appointed Forest Ranger to succeed Ray King, resigned, has arrived and taken up the work at the local station. He comes from Canjilion—where he had been employed by the Carson NF.

In 1922 **W.H. Woods, Jr**. was living in High Rolls and became one of the first rangers on the Gallinas National Forest. He went on to become the Supervisor of the Coronado NF in 1955 and Forest Supervisor of the Crook NF in Safford, Arizona.

John H. Mims – Alamogordo News—1923—the Lincoln Forest Supervisor O. Fred Arthur was in Corona with Gallinas Ranger J.H. Mims surveying the Gallinas Mountain Reserve. Earlier in the month Mims had to leave his duty station and drive to Carrizozo as one of his children was sick.

EUEL R. NAVE 1951-1955

42

Euel R. Nave served as the Mountainair District Ranger from 1951-1955. Euel was born in Arkansas in 1902, but his family moved to Monticello (near Truth or Consequences) when he was young. He was one of the founders of the New Mexico Forestry Department. He worked for the U.S. Forest Service until his retirement. Afterwards, he and his wife Ruby took over operation of the Coalson Ranch near Hillsboro.

Vincent R. Price served as the District Ranger for only one year between 1957 and 1958. Vince found his calling early in life and he graduated from the University of Berkeley in 1952 with a forestry degree. His fulfilling career with the Forest Service took Vince around the country fighting fires and working in land management. In 1964 he was transferred to Missoula, Montana where he served as the assistant director of recreation and lands. He retired in 1985 at the age of 55 to pursue his passion for hunting and fishing.

Susan A. Gray was the Mountainair District's first woman District Ranger although she only remained in that position for one year between 1988 and 1989. She worked on a brochure on rights for women working for the U.S. Forest Service.

Frank Martinez (Article in the Mountain Times in July of 2005) Frank Martinez has been the District Ranger here at the Sacramento District for the last four years and 11 years prior to that on the Mountainair District of the Cibola NF. Frank was drawn to the role of district ranger by this desire to make a difference on the ground with the belief that there is truly no better job in the agency than to work as a district ranger.

Vicky Estrada served as Mountainair's second woman District Ranger. During Estrada's term as District Ranger she instituted the Las Humanas Project. This project was a partnership between the U.S. Forest Service and locals living within one of four land grants in the area.

In 1999, Las Humanas entered into an agreement with the Forest Service for a 120-acre thinning project to reduce the fire risk around local communities. In 2001, the local Forest Service District developed a plan for a 10,000-acre restoration project in the Manzano Mountains—the Thunderbird Project.

Karen Lessard came to the Mountainair District in 2007 from the Los Angeles National Forest in California. She grew up in Portland, Maine and received a forestry degree from the University of New Hampshire.

Karen always wanted to become a forest ranger. When she was a kid she watched Lassie and Ranger Corey. She thought Ranger Corey had the best job and she told her father that she planned on becoming a forest ranger. He told her that girls did not go into that field and she should find another interest, as she would have a hard time finding a job.

Karen worked in many different fields before assuming the responsibilities as the District Ranger at Mountainair. For many years, she worked as a back country ranger and spent most of her week patrolling on foot throughout the mountains. This was one of her favorite positions before becoming the District Ranger.

KAREN LESSARD DISTRICT RANGER 2007-2015

MOUNTAINAIR JOB CORPS CENTER & THE CONSTRUCTION OF THE MOUNTAINAIR RANGER STATION

The Mountainair Job Corps Center is all but forgotten, but when it first came to town in 1965, it was a big deal to the residents of Mountainair and Torrance County. Several hundred people waited at the train depot in Mountainair to welcome the first 23 corpsmen to town on April 22, 1965. The high school band played as they descended from the train.

The Job Corps system decided to close their conservation centers in New Mexico and operate two camps at Alpine and Heber in Arizona in 1969.

Corpsmen built a new ranger station, shop and barn for the Mountainair Ranger District that is still used by the District today.

History of the Mountainair, NM Ranger District
U.S. Forest Service Photos
Copyright © 2016 Dixie Boyle
All Rights Reserved